BE
OUTSTANDING

Contents

How to use this book 4

About the Authors 5

About Yogarten 7

INTRODUCTION 8

   Accepting The Gift.. 8

Chapter 1- Letting go 10

   Intro – The lizard and you.. 10

   Personal Development – A lighthearted attitude 14

   Yoga – Breath energy and relaxation............................. 23

   Art – The beauty of tension..................................... 29

Chapter 2 - Rise and shine... 40

   Intro – The authentic you 40

   Personal Development – The image of the mind......... 42

   Yoga – The mind movie.. 53

   Art – The letter and the portrait 59

Chapter 3–A real treat.. 66

   Intro – The opposite of work...................................... 66

   Personal Development–Changing perspective 68

   Yoga – Moving into happiness 74

   Art – Zen Madala a pattern of beauty 80

Chapter 4 Shaping success 87

   Intro – Embrace your intuition 87

   Personal Development –Ask and receive..................... 89

Yoga- Worshipping the sun 96

Art –Starting to flow 99

Chapter 5 –Have fun! 105

Intro- Cultivating individuality 105

Personal Development – Faux fun and real fun 108

Yoga – Connect to the heart 115

Art –Tap in your creative force 117

CONCLUSION 125

How to use this book

"In theory there is no difference between theory and practice. In practice there is." - Yogi Berra

Outstanding impliesbeing unique, have skills, expertise or knowledge to add additional value and become indispensable. We simply need to be outstanding! You have to figure out ways to distinguish yourself from everyone else. In our daily life and routines it is sometimes hard to leave our own patterns of thinking,yet we have to do it in order to grow and flourish and sustain our career.

We often come to our own boundaries and think they are fixed. When we are able to step out of our head, we realize that there are potentials within ourselves that we may not have expected. We often experience this after a vacation. Our horizon is open, and we gained strength to conquer new challenges. Unfortunately, we don't always have the time to go on vacation instantly and recharge when we need it.

Art and Yoga give you the opportunity to recharge sustainably. In this book, we areusing the same methods we are using during our retreats to create an outstanding life for our clients. To grant you this wholesome and holistic experience, each chapter is divided into four parts:

1. The Intro: A short overview
2. Personal Development: The profound theories for intellectual understanding.
3. Yoga: The Yoga exercises give you the opportunity to experience this information on an emotional/bodily level and offers tools to overcome obstacles,
4. Art: The art exercises lets the theory and the bodily experience manifest in a beautiful artwork. This can serve as a beautiful reminder, artwork for your home or office or even as beautiful gift for someone who deserves it.

Be open, curious and playful! Allow yourself to experience with your mind, body and soul. Enjoy the journey. This book gives you the opportunity to become outstanding.

About the Authors

Heinrich is a source of creativity whether it manifests in paintings, photography, books or videos the media are manifold. Since his birth Heinrich has always been creative even a short detour with a military career lead him back to creativity and he became a front photographer. His love of art, and wish to share cultural values was the reason to found his own art academy. When Heinrich isn't teaching he is creating.

With over a decade of experience in assisting a management director Janaki (Janine)knows how rewarding, yet demanding, this position can be. Since the beginning of her Yoga practice she integrated practice and theory in her daily life. These ancient practices, adapted to today's life, increase the life quality tremendously. Yoga isn't just about the poses which are often presented in a sometimes sportive,inaccessible way. From the beginning of her yogic path, it was her aim to bring relaxation, peace of mind and overall well-being to her students, knowing that some things cannot be bought.

Heinrich's art school and gallery served as a Yoga studio. Art students joined the Yoga classes and reported positive effects theYoga had on their creativity. On the other hand,Yoga students from the business world started to discover their creative side and joined art classes next to the Yoga classes. The art and Yoga fusion idea was born.Together they developed a program that helps working women connect with their creativity in a way that will benefit their careers.

Heinrich and Janaki will always remain students.When they are not teaching, they travel the world to learn and bring their knowledge back to their students.

About Yogarten

Yogarten developed the Yoga and art fusion to describe the innovative integration of mind and body with the practice of self-development. Yogarten takes high performers on a journey to a new level that promises and delivers on better quality of life using the ancient wisdom of art and Yoga, combined with personal development.

INTRODUCTION
Accepting The Gift

"To give anything less than your best, is to sacrifice the gift." - Steve Prefontaine

You are gifted. You are talented. You have the potential to achieve great things. You have strengths and talents which can make a difference in the world. You were given life for a purpose.

Perhaps you feel that you have not been blessed with any particular gifts but relax, the truth is that you have just not yet discovered what they are. For example, A beautiful girl can look in the mirror daily and consider herself ugly, a talented musician may think that they are no good at becoming one with their instrument of choice. It is through searching and demolishing obstacles along the journey to which you have been called that will reveal your true gift.

There are times when we are active in our pursuit of excellence, and just the thought of being good at something for once in our lives greatly empowers us to find who we really are. At other times we push really hard but become mentally and physically exhausted when we cannot reach our perceived goals. The world is a busy place. The noise and the rush and push , leave little space to have a free mind. Yet in order to unlock our true potential, we need to stop, we need to rest and we need to listen to what our bodies and minds are telling us to do.

Aimlessly pushing yourself into changes and situations which you are not conditioned towards will have a counterproductive effect, leaving you frustrated. Take time to discover your gift and then evaluate it. Self validation is key, look at where you are now and set goals for what you want to achieve. Loosen up by taking an art class or going for a good run, but most importantly, consider what you can learn from the incorporation of Yoga and Art into your day to day activities.

Chapter 1- Letting go

Intro – The lizard and you

Becoming all that you were created to be not only requires you to be bold and creative, you also need to release all of the tension and doubt you are feeling so that you can become your best self. However, don't feel as though you are defeated or unworthy when you crash and burn under difficult situations or even become shy to the extent of trembling and sweating profusely. It is all a part of our carnal nature as human beings. Have you heard of the "lizard brain"? This is an actual physical part of your brain. It is responsible for generating primal fears such as pain, anger and hunger. Although these emotions are of great necessity, they may also cause damage by invoking emotions which may hinder our progression to our true selves. The lizard brain is often the reason why we say we want one thing and then do another. It is why we attend a job interview but then commit self sabotage. Therefore we need to find a way to silence the lizard and strive for our goals undistorted by fear or worry.

Most of us were brought up with the mentality that we are to unrelentingly pursue our dreams and achieve great things; we should eat healthy, be well prepared for exams, keep our bodies healthy and be ambitious. Although all of this is important, remember that you are control of your life and you can make choices which directly effect how you live it.

Get up and boldly go after your dreams, and do not be confined by the opinions of others or even the fear of not meeting their expectations. As was said before, you are enough and your daily pursuit should be to become a better you, as opposed to competing with anyone. This is not to say that at times we will not feel intimidated or that we have not accomplished enough when we compare ourselves with others facing similar circumstances as us. The reality of life is that the grass may seem greener from your perspective, but the reality may not always be as perfect as the idea seems.

The main idea of living a utopian lifestyle is that we may be freed from the things which we fear the most such as: criticism from those who we love and adore, and even judgment and blame which may be inflicted by others. Not only can this fear of not being perfect drive you to become someone you are not, it would undoubtedly stifle the beautiful and amazing person you are. The world needs you to perform and contribute in the manner which you were created. So although acceptance from others may seem like the world to some, it certainly takes a toll and depletes self-worth and acceptance.

Personal Development – A lighthearted attitude

"Tension is who you think you should be, relaxation is who you are." – Chinese proverb

Have you been tense lately? Do you just work, work, work; come home and do chores, take care of everyone else and just simply put yourself on the back burner? As previously mentioned, it is essential to your health and well-being to relax and rejuvenate yourself for all the foreseeable and unforeseeable "surprises" this life may have in store for you! If you find that you get tense often and take little to no time to relax, or maintain, this could be a key indication that you are pretty stressed out, to say the least.

Life is always going to throw undesirable events at you to catch you off guard, and you need to be prepared and focused to endure. Some key signs of an increased stress level include: muscle aches and pains, migraines, fatigue, poor decision making, low quality of work, low energy, tendency to avoid others, increased errors, among others. In addition to the aforementioned, behavioral changes may be observed, such as eating alone, low self-confidence, lack of interest in things that were once fascinating and an overall lack of enthusiasm toward life.

Now that you may have come to acknowledge how some of the physical things you are experiencing might just be an outward sign of your emotions and mentality, here are my suggestions on how this stress may be reduced and even combated all together.

You, like many others, may be interested in lowering your tension so that you may better manage obstacles or challenges that will most definitely come your way. However, the resolution of this problem doesn't necessarily lie within the realm of the problem itself, but rather your reaction toward the problem. There is a solution and one that you most definitely will be able to achieve if you make up your mind and bravely decide to tackle whatever may come your way. Of course, that last sentence sounded great, but the truth of the matter is that it is way more adrenaline pumping and tedious than the words you just read; but it can change your life!

Take my advice, try adopting an attitude of lightheartedness, find the fun in the simple things when it is hard for you to be at peace with the more technical and complex changes in your life. At the end of the day, you most definitely will not be able to change the predicaments in your life, sometimes you will just have to keep walking until you see your way through. But in between the heartache and the things that really hurt you to your core, intentionally seek to find the joy in things, and if you can't spot an ounce of joy from your perspective, simply create some!

Achieving optimal success should not only be measured by the financial wealth which you accumulate; the magnitude of success rests on the life you lead and your ability to be diverse enough to handle whatever challenges may come your way. For some of us, we may actually be basking in a successful life, but we are too busy trying to keep things in order that we don't ever take a minute to stop and just enjoy what we currently have; there's always something else to achieve, something else to purchase, something else to do! It is strongly suggested that by incorporating relaxing practices such as Yoga and art into your daily life, you may in fact place yourself on a path flooding with ways in which you may better manage success. In this sense, success being health, joy, happiness, and a sense of true satisfaction.

During hard times, it will almost seem natural to have a bad attitude and outlook. Something as simple as a smile from another person will rock your core to wrath, and cause that inner-void of happiness and anger to brew into something incredibly nasty that you never knew you were capable of becoming.

Take the time to meditate on whether you are doing all that you can do to heal yourself. Are you doing all that you can do? Are you making a deliberate effort to change the things you can, while you are waiting for those which you cannot control to pass? Are you loving yourself? Are you taking care of your mind, body and soul? Are you treating yourself the way you wish others would treat you? Yes, we require so much validation from others and we are upset and mad when they don't treat us the way we deserve to be treated. But are you treating yourself the way you want them to treat you?

It is often mind-blowing that we go the extra mile for others, yet we neglect ourselves in the process. We fail to acknowledge the connection between how we treat ourselves and how others will treat us. Come to the realization that the things you accept and the way you allow other individuals to treat you may be a direct reflection of the disservice you are doing to yourself! How can you correct this? Teach others how to treat you!

One point which you may find to be greatly fascinating is the fact that we were raised to believe that we are naturally the way we are and there is nothing that we can ever do to change that. However, the truth is that our personality has the ability to influence our attitude and the way which we perceive ourselves and the ways others perceive us. In light of this, it is necessary to highlight the different personalities which people may have.

Some individuals are quiet and tend to take just about everything seriously. It is no surprise that these same individuals may always behave as though they are in deep though and constantly worried about something. Socializing may also be an enormous issue for these individuals, which ties back to the fear and worry of the virtually impossible.

On the other hand, the complete opposite is also heavily present in our society. Some people tend to have no composure at all and are always on a never-ending pursuit to create amazing social experiences and having a great time; with little or no concern for maintaining a good job and aspiring to be a contributing member to a hard-working society. Additionally, these individuals normally complete all the tasks they set out to achieve in a playful and jocular manner, which others may perceive as inappropriate or simply childish.

With that being said, the ultimate goal which should be sought after is the creation of a balance between both mannerisms. Undoubtedly, both have their benefits and disadvantages, and the goal should be to maximize on the benefits of each class of conduct without overly indulging to the point of your own demise.

There are many benefits to living an easy-going life and approaching situations with a lighthearted and playful attitude. Not only can you improve on your emotional health, you may also form friendships which may have never materialized otherwise because of your previous attitude. Positive experiences may also be enhance by the creation of such a great attitude toward life that you are able to identify even more things to be happy and grateful for, regardless of how small the beneficial pleasure may be.

Conversely, if you let go of the reins and allow your life to be filled with negative influences everywhere you turn, you may find that you are hard to converse with, rigorous, strict and welcoming to even more negativity! This is pretty much common sense if you think about it, and when you acknowledge the truth of this explanation, you are even more empowered to look out for ways in which you can change for the better.

This doesn't necessarily mean that you will end up leading a boring life, or on the other extreme, a wild life packed with tons of reckless behaviors. You can still live the life of your dreams and participate in the things that you love. What is vital to its sustenance is the elimination of negative drama and intensity by the elimination of people, things and foreseeable challenges that have the potential of disturbing the peace of mind that you have worked so assiduously to achieve. Open yourself to life, and embrace moments without worrying about ridiculous things. Try to ignore the sometimes dysfunctional need to control others around you. Get into the habit of treating yourself the way you need to be treated. Make it a point of duty to take care of yourself without all the guilt and negative thinking! You may find that you are comparing yourself to the lives of others, and based on their actions, you build your life around what you think they would allow in their own lives. Two words: STOP IT! You are your own person; you have your own brain. Stop seeking false validation and reassurance, it is not secure.

Start envisioning yourself as strong and powerful, identify the things and people in your life that are hindering you from becoming your best self and ability to live a constructive, happy life!

With enough practice, you'll eventually figure out that creating balance in your life is the best strategy, and that worrying and obsessing isn't going to help anything but rob you of your health and of the precious and happy moments and opportunities that you could have had, if you'd only approached things with a lighthearted and positive attitude. Choosing to focus more on the lighter side of life won't resolve all of your problems, but it can definitively make you feel better, and that can lead to living a happy and more fulfilled life. It's your choice, so choose wisely.

It is imperative to place yourself in positive situations as often as possible. Try spending more time doing the things that you enjoy. A lot of your day-to-day activities and situations maybe boring, but you can turn most of them into positive experiences by simply maintaining a lighthearted and easygoing attitude.

Ask yourself "Am I giving too much of myself to others and not enough for myself?", "Do I need to take time to pamper myself?", If the answers are "yes" refuse to feel guilty about it and do it!

Do something good for yourself, enjoy every single minute of it and tell the negative party meeting in your head to shut up! Free yourself from your own negativity, and go out and do the things you love! No regrets!

Yoga – Breath energy and relaxation

"Every breath we take, every step we make, can be filled with peace, joy and serenity." - Thich Nhat Hanh

A number of studies conducted on the effect of Yoga on stress and anxiety have provided results which have concluded that Yoga is indeed greatly influential in reducing stress and anxiety. Yoga may be exemplified as the connection of the spirit to the body in a way that not only provides great exercise, but also releases stress and confusion from the body, through a series of planned poses and breathing exercises. It has also be posited that breathing healthy not only helps you to live longer, but may also provide drastic increase in your overall mood and mannerisms. Our energy levels depend greatly on our ability to breathe, so, the better and deeper you breather, the more energy you are likely to have.

Learning to breathe

Controlled breathing not only keeps the mind and body functioning at their best, it can also lower blood pressure, promote feelings of calmness and relaxation and help us de-stress and calms the mind.

Many of my students come to my classes because they are tired, stressed and sometimes anxious. On one occasion, Susan asked why she can totally let go after Yoga exercises, but she can never sleep or relax during the day at home. I told her it is because of the breath work we have previously done. Once she realized that it was her breathing she started to apply it to her daily life!

I learned the breathing techniques in an Ashram in India, and watched many students closely on their journey. I have observed mouth breathers, shallow breathers and even experts in natural breathing.

It is often thought that we need a completely quiet place to relax and release tension. No doubt we need a vacation from time to time, but you should not be trying to run away from your life! By practicing some simple breathing techniques, you may learn how to ease tension and gradually change your mood in the blink of an eye without drawing unwanted attention to yourself. You may inhale, exhale and retain your breathing, it may sound like nothing spectacular, but you may be surprised at how well you feel subsequent to mastering control of your respiratory and nervous systems.

You will learn more beneficial breathing techniques and also be introduced to step- by- step breathing patterns which may raise your energy levels or calm your mind.

You have sufficient knowledge of breathing since you have been doing it since the moment you were born, there's nothing you can't learn!

<u>Yoga Breathing exercise</u>

Have you ever thought about your breathing? Not really right? Breathing happens automatically and we can be happy it does. Just imagine what would happen if you would be responsible for every inhale and exhale...

The autonomic nervous system is responsible for the involuntary functions of the human body - this includes your breathing. It is divided in the Parasympathetic Nervous System (PNS) and Sympathetic Nervous System (SNS). Breathing is the only automatic function that you can control at will. This can be used like a manual override and you can influence your whole nervous system. By proper breathing you can relax your whole nervous system.

Our mind and our breath are connected with each other. When we are stressed or feel threatened, our breathing becomes rapid and short. When we are relaxed our breathing is slow and deep. Here is a test to proof it. Ask someone to listen closely to a noise: Do you here the ambulance? Watch closely the person will hold the breath while trying to hear noise. Or watch yourself, when you want to thread a needle you hold your breath while being concentrated. You can see that the mind influences the breath and the breath influences the mind.

That's the reason why you can use your breath to relax.

But what exactly is proper breathing?

Nobody taught us how to breathe. Babies breathe properly through the nose only and all the incoming air goes down in the belly. That is called Diaphragmatic breathing.

There are many reason why we don't breathe deep in the belly.

1. The area is restricted through clothing. Tight pants and belts.

2. Posture. Rounded upper back so that we breathe only in the chest area.
3. Overeating.
4. We dont like to feel the belly area not even to mention an extend belly... But why? Nobody will watch your belly during a conversation nor even notice at all that it goes in and out.

Why through the nose?

When we breathe through the nose, the incoming air gets warmed up and filtered through the nostrils.

What is diaphragmatic breathing?

The diaphragm is the muscle beneath your lungs that helps you breathe. To practice it is best to lie on the floor. Place your hand on your stomach on your navel. Now start to breathe normally and watch your hand. You might see it move only a bit. When you breathe properly your belly will go out on the inhale because your diaphragm descends and when you exhale your belly goes in because your diaphragm ascends. This can take some practice but keep at it and you will get it. Try to breathe the same way without using your hand. Once you got it you can practice it sitting.

Working with this actively can be particularly effective in reducing anxiety.

Have you ever heard your breath?

That was the first questions my Yoga teacher in India asked me. My honest answer was: "No". If your answer is no too, let's do what I have to do. No we get really scientific. Plug your ears with your index fingers and start to breathe through your nose. Take a couple of breath. You can close your eyes if you want to. What do you hear? I hear the ocean and my breath are the weaves. Some of my students hear tree leaves in the wind or just the wind.

Here is an exercise that you can do anywhere. Use the diaphragmatic breath and concentrate on the sound. Now inhale and count in your head 1,2,3,4 then exhale and count again 1,2,3,4. After a couple of rounds you will feel that your mind is calmer. When you exhale longer than you inhale, for example inhale 1,2 exhale 1,2,3,4 you activate the PNS and this exercise will calm your nervous system.

Art – The beauty of tension

"Colors, like features, follow the changes of the emotions." - Pablo Picasso

By participating in artistic activities and bodily exercise, regardless of form, has the potential to make us more easy-going and acceptable of the circumstances which may arise in our lives. These actions may also relieve tension as it actually causes the individual to see the problem not as the actual existent problem, but how they react to it. When your mind is at ease and able to think rationally, it is no doubt that being distracted by minor worries or overreacting to situations which may be easily rectified can be diminished.

But can we use tension itself as a vehicle to relive stress and create with this something beautiful? First of all tension and stress is not a bad thing and also what do we mean when we say that a particular work of art is beautiful? As human beings, our sensory receptors enable most of us to find similar things gratifying.

We all tend to find the same kinds of things

beautiful, sunsets for example and their brilliant panoply of color, or the haunting songs of birds, or perhaps the curve of warm marble lying in the sun, all these things and many more are recreated in art and it is the power and wonder of such recreation that makes art beautiful to us. The tension speaks about the good and the bad, the easy and the difficult in life. Art that is happy all the time like elevator music, flower-print wallpaper, and smiley-face designs are not necessarily good works of art. Good art often is filled with tension and the ability to evoke emotion.

Why tension? You may ask. Our own lives are filled with opposites which are consistently struggling to gain power over the opposition. We describe our emotional lives in terms of opposites: happy, sad; angry, passionate; crying, laughing. Good pieces of art allows us to feel the emotions which are connected to different happenings in our lives, whether good or bad, and conditions us on how to accept happiness and disappointment. This is exactly why art is a spectacular language which is used by every single creature you can think of to communicate with the world at large.

Notwithstanding this, the so-called tension and ugliness which is sometimes identifiable in glorified pieces may be classified as good art, although we might never ever want to come into contact with those visually stimulating pieces for as long as breath resides in our bodies. The contradictions and inconsistencies which are depicted might be so provocative to our minds that they arouse buried memories and the bitter ugly residue of our past. However, the same art which rips the bandage off the wound, and allows for a painful experience from exposure, allows for the cooling and soothing winds to heal and restore what was once damaged or lost.

One great solution for avoiding a life of misery from the nuances that are going to appear in life is to embrace the presence of tension, use it to your advantage and go into each day with tension labeled as a learning experience. By utilizing the creative process of art and having low tolerance for the entry and growth of negativity, even the most vulnerable individuals who are usually less comfortable and capable of expressing themselves through words may develop a great sense of self.

One of my students, Arthur, was in the aforementioned position and completely unable to see himself for the great person that others saw him to be. Working in a very tense business environment, art could most definitely help achieve equilibrium with the processing of his thoughts and emotions, thus catapulting him to achieving his full potential. It is most definitely my pleasure to be able to guide my clients through these processes of creative expression; which unbeknownst to many takes a great load off their shoulders, one which was probably carried for innumerable years.

For me, subsequent to completing time in the military I experienced Post-traumatic Stress Disorder (PTSD) and was constantly trying to search for everything I could possibly understand about this disorder. Most of my time was spent being stressed out and extremely stressed from the hyper vigilant behavior I was expressing. We may not notice, but underneath this habit of watching our surroundings is a kind of wild, scary feeling of searching for and seeking potential danger. It doesn't matter if we know intellectually that we are no longer in danger because this is originating from an unconscious, instinctual and animalistic part of ourselves. It's like we have a wild animal eye attached to us that is always stuck wide open; like a sentry always at the ready even if nothing is there anymore. For me art was the way out. I was happy to meet an artist and he showed me the benefits of participating in these activities. Instead of defining myself as tense, stressed and anxious, I could rewire myself to be aware of every moment and actually chose to enjoy it.

As you can clearly see, tension may be utilized to bring about positivity in your life! Let's now take a deeper look at the myth which states that art has to be harmonious to be beautiful. It is often in the midst of chaos that the most astonishing discoveries are unveiled. Nature has a funny way of showcasing that rare beauties can be birthed out of messes. The idea of harmony in all situations is very utopian and in really, life doesn't just work that way! If the utopian would have their way, diamonds would have probably never existed as it is only when certain elements are placed under pressure that they transform to create what we know as the cherished diamond.

We can most definitely use tension to create our own masterpiece!The main purpose of the exercise is to encourage you to view stress objectively as a means by which you can use stress and tension for the benefit of your life, as opposed to behaving in a frantic and fearful manner over every little trial that may come your way. Don't get me wrong, it is completely necessary that you are mindful of what is going on around you but you need not be on alert; awareness is key!

Secondly, being content with your present situation at all levels of your mind, body and soul is certainly important to ensure that you are in a safe mental place with the ability to utilize whatever may come your way. Don't be shy to sit and meditate on your relationship with yourself, connect with the inner you and this will open up a great array of possibilities. So, let's begin:

1. First write down the good and bad feelings that you experience and try to find a color that will fit this feeling.
2. Relax your body and eyes.
3. Slow down your attempts to get information out of the environment around you.
4. Notice the environment in a calm way.
5. Pull all of your attention inside your body.
6. Ask yourself the following questions about your body:
   i. Which parts of my body feel the light like air?
   ii. Where can I feel energy and heat?
   iii.Where isthe tension and pressure located?

These exercises usually go from the body's surface where we usually experience pressure and air, and advances to the muscles where tension is usually felt and where the most heat in the body is present and less likely to allow for the detection of tension. After going through the above steps, it is essential that you transform your view of the environment and perceive it from a calm and collected place. Then you will notice that you can be calm and receptive at the same time before being overly alert and irrational.

Now we can get to the fun part, we can transform this into a work of art.

1. Pick your colors and link them to your feelings and experiences.

2. If you want to make a small artwork, draw the shape of a body on a piece of paper and color every section of your body with the color that you are experiencing in different parts or sections of your body.A masterpiece is lying down on a canvas and letting someone draw the shape of your body on the canvas. If you have a little more time feel free to make two shapes, one that represents how you feel and one in which you choose the colors of how you wish to feel.

3. To take this exercise to the next level of fun let's turn this into a messy painting exercise.

Why do I call this the messy painting exercise?
Forget your nails and definitely wear old clothes.

In this exercise, you'll explore and play with all your
materials, so there's no right or wrong way to
proceed. It's all about your feelings, you won't try to
make anything specific, and that takes the pressure
off. If a subject evolves, that's great. Get ready and
line up items that you will need, they may include:
liquid gesso and a spray bottle loaded with rubbing
alcohol, newspapers, pieces of cut mat board and
corrugated cardboard, a linoleum stamp, paper
towels, tissues and old towels for wiping.

Here's one way to start.

1. Pour or squirt fluid paint like acrylic into a
   little matte medium you've applied at random
   to the paper.
2. After squirting, take a big brush and mix all
   the paint and the matte medium together.
   Immediately manipulate the paint by lifting
   off with a tissue and drawing into the paint
   with your brush handle end later stamping
   into the messy mixture.
3. Keep the paint moving by wetting your brush
   and bringing some of the mixture down the
   paper.

With a brayer, roll through the initial mixture, and then quickly roll the brayer over a section of the paper that hasn't been painted.

4. Cover the rest of the paper with brushstrokes of various sizes, using all the original paints you squirted. Let the painting dry completely after you've covered the paper.
   When you return to the painting, stamp, draw and paint opaque passages, and then stop to assess.

5. If you have a good abstract painting that represents your initial feelings with the LET exercise, stop! If not, let the painting dry and then apply a veil of white gesso (liquid gesso thinned with water) over the surface.
   Drawing the small shapes in a notebook can also become your diary of feelings.

Relief through abstract paintings about your inner state can be helpful in dealing with stress.Hyper vigilance develops subconsciously during tense situations and can gradually cause damage to your health in the long run. Virtually any form of exercise, from aerobics to Yoga, can act as a stress reliever. If you're not an athlete or if you're out of shape, you can still make a little exercise go a long way toward stress management.

Try to discover the connection between exercise and stress relief and why exercise should be part of your stress management plan. Exercise increases your overall health and your sense of well-being but it also has some direct stress-busting benefits and it includes pumping up your endorphins, your brain's feel-good neurotransmitters. Although this function is often referred to as a runner's high, a rousing game of tennis or a nature hike can also contribute to this type of feeling.

After a fast-paced game of racquetball or several laps in the pool, you'll often find that you've forgotten the day's irritations and concentrate only on your body's movements. As you begin to regularly shed your daily tensions through movement and physical activity, you may find that you focus on a single task, and the resulting energy and optimism, can help you remain calm and clear in everything you do. Regular exercise can further increase self-confidence, relax you, enhance sleep, and can even lower the symptoms associated with mild depression and anxiety.

Chapter 2 - Rise and shine

Intro – The authentic you

Authenticity is a choice that requires courage, compassion and connection. Most people would like to live a life that is true to who they are; in other words, we'd all like to be as authentic as possible. Unfortunately, a handful of factors stand in the way of this; the most prominent being a lack of self-confidence. In light of this, we may feel as though we are not true to ourselves, and it may even cause us to question the relationships and friendships which we have maintained for decades. Am I really who they think I am? Do I even accept me? Are just a few of the deeply intriguing questions we may ask ourselves when we are weakened by our ability to see past the fact that at one point or another we all lose ourselves and it is through the journey of loss that we naturally strive to uncover who we are.

At the end of the day, authenticity isn't actually a quality that you either have or you don't; it is a conscious and intentional choice that is merely an outward sign of our inward desire to become our best self. Seeing that it is actually a choice, we have the option of deciding whether we concede to the norms and values which have been set out for us by our predecessors or whether we are going to be less authentic on other days. Regardless of whatever side we choose on whichever day, once we have life and a new day, we may attempt to alter our previous decisions, so as to find a common ground which is suitable not only for our conscience but also one that will make those around us feel comfortable and at ease.

For instance, if an employee sees his / her work as frustrating and not motivational, the lack of motivation will be noticed by management, and when times get tough, he/she will be the first to be fired. However, there is always the option of learning from yesterday and adapting to changes which will provide for a better tomorrow. Another common misconception that is always dwindling over the heads of those which are in lower ranks is that they don't have the resources to be outstanding and creative.One of the most life-changing lines you might ever read in this book is this; there is only one of you in this entire world! Even if you are a twin or triplet, there is no one that is exactly like you in every single sense of the word. Use this to your advantage!

Personal Development – The image of the mind

"Thoughts live; they travel far." - Swami
Vivekananda

It is important that you feel good about yourself.
More and more scientific evidence keeps pointing
toward a significant link between how you feel
about yourself and your overall health and sense of
well-being. Scientists have consistently proven that
feelings of inferiority have the capacity to pave the
way to illness or disease. On the other hand, if you
feel good about yourself, have a positive outlook,
and maintain active involvement in your daily life,
then there is a great likelihood that you'll be more
happy and healthy.

It is impossible for anyone to feel perfectly happy
about who he is for their entire life. We are all bound
to feel inferior or insecure once in a while.
Fortunately, our thoughts and feelings are not
permanent and there are so many ways to love,
accept and feel good about ourselves. If you can
begin to change some of the smaller thoughts and
emotions by realizing that your brain can produce
just about anything it conceives, then you can learn

how to change the larger thoughts and emotions you experience.

You Have The Power To Determine Your Thoughts

Lack of self-awareness is one of the primary reasons why individuals feel as though they have no control over the sad and depressing thoughts that flush their minds at some point or another. We often feel like there is no way to bypass this messed up way of thinking, and instead allow ourselves to just take whatever grows roots into our minds, hoping that eventually it will subside and give us a renewed sense of peace. This impression is a complete fallacy and one which can be changed with swift action and relentless pursuit. Could it be that the problems you are currently experiencing aren't necessarily the "problem"? What if the problem is how you relate to yourself? The way you buy into those negative thoughts? This is not to say that you are expected to be flawless and without error, but from a literal perspective, how do you know that the little thoughts moving around in your mind and possibly wreaking havoc on your physical body aren't just thoughts? Thoughts which you have the power to change to anything you want them to be! Is it possible that you are being troubled by mere thoughts which are highly unlikely to develop into real life events? Think about it!

Do yourself a favor and stop striving after what society may portray to you as the norm and allow your mind, body and soul to lead you on a journey to becoming yourself and not just mirroring anybody else.

Quite a number of students who have come to us for assistance have struggled for years with low self-esteem issues. Many times, they may feel as though their efforts to become a better person are futile, and even if they do engage in some rewarding activities, the pleasure is short-lived and soon the feelings of inadequacy and lack of importance return to assume what may be considered their right place. It may even be of great surprise to you that the number of successful individuals who may be viewed to engage in satisfying and progressive work, are often troubled deep down inside by what we may consider to be subordinate to their actual accomplishments.

You may feel like a schmuck because you may feel your thighs are too large, when in fact you are a home owner, you're in a stable and highly-ranked job, you can vacation twice a year, you own a luxury vehicle and you're about to start a family. It is simply amazing that although we have done so much, in comparison to minor dislikes regarding our bodies or whatever other area of our lives, we seem to feed the negativity to the point where all we have ever worked for is basically worth nothing because of that miniscule thing that just absolutely gets on our nerves.

A great advantage of art and Yoga is that it is an experimental field without consequences when we change our mindset. In everyday life what we may not be aware of is that achieving our image of success doesn't effectively change our emotional state. It doesn't do anything to permanently change the way the voice in our head speaks to us or what we believe about ourselves. Many times people have achieved their goals only to find themselves still unfulfilled. Your emotional state may briefly change if there is success in an aspect of your life, but the core belief of not being good enough and your long term habit of self-rejectionhasn't really been altered. The critical voice in our head is more likely to put a higher goal in front of us to achieve.

I was working with a manager once, who had achieved her financial dreams several years back, but, surprisingly, she described the achievement like a failure because she was only ranked about 10th in a list of the most successful business women in her niche. Though it's okay to have high goals, it is important to realize that you don't have to make your love and self-acceptance dependent on them; stop being overly critical of yourself and just strive to feel good about who you are.

I myself tried to fix my own self-esteem issues, but they didn't work out as I thought they would, so I thought; why not try something different? Instead of indulging in negative thoughts about myself, I acknowledge them as just thoughts, which may or may not be true. One technique that has worked for me is just to see thoughts as just thoughts, and always remembering that feelings and emotions can change in the blink of an eye as they are only temporary.

The approach of dissolving the image of ourselves and perfection may sound contrary to our sense of logic about building confidence and esteem. This is because we have the belief that achieving the image of perfection will result in positive and happy emotions and feelings contingent with our success. Since our childhood, our minds have actually been programmed to have these emotional associations. We desire to feel these feelings and chase the image of perfection we have attached to them. Sadly, more often than not, we end up with the opposing outcome than what is expected.

Below are some steps which will help you to bolster your feelings regarding self-worth.

Step 1: Reframe Your Identity

If you were asked to describe yourself, what would you say? What would be the first adjectives that you would come to your mind? Experts say that a person's self-worth can be assessed by the first five words that he would use to answer this question. If you answer with negative adjectives, then you would need to redefine how you think about yourself.

Instead of focusing on the shortfalls in your life, try to bring to mind things that make you special. For example, instead of branding yourself as a mere slave of your bad habits, try looking at yourself as someone who is in a learning process, and pride yourself on your greatest achievements instead of highlighting your flaws or mistakes.

Step 2: Challenge Negative Self-Talk

As we go about our daily lives, we constantly think about and interpret every situation that we encounter. It's like we have this voice inside our head that talks us through everything which we come into contact with. Psychologists call this the inner voice, but it could also be referred to as self-talk.

How our inner voice talks to us is based on our values, beliefs and our conscious and subconscious thoughts. If your self-talk is mostly negative, you will have a very hard time feeling good about yourself. To correct negative self-talk, you need to learn to notice it as it happens, and consciously dispute and challenge these negative and irrational thoughts. Ask yourself questions like, "Are my thoughts factual?" ,"Is this situation as bad as I am making out to be?" or "What can I do that will help me solve the problem?" Make it a point to conquer self-defeating thoughts with positive and realistic ways of thinking.

Step 3: Take Time For Yourself

In a world where everyone and everything seems to be in a rush, most of us don't make ourselves a priority. Often we focus on catering to the needs of others and on being productive. Although it is good to take care of the people you love and fulfill your responsibilities at home and at work, you should not neglect your responsibility and obligations to yourself.

Changing how you feel emotionally starts with recognizing beliefs and thoughts which you give much energy to in your mind. Always try to allocate a certain amount of time each day for yourself to do things you love. Give yourself some "you time" to do things which you love, as this has been proven to improve self-esteem and feelings of self-worth.

Identifying your beliefs will better enable you to change how you feel emotionally, while helping you to avoid beliefs that will create emotions of insecurity and fear. The emotions are not the problem; they are just the symptoms of negative core beliefs. The "not good enough" image is as a result of our imagination and belief. These are beliefs about ourselves created by the mind concluding that we are "not good enough to meet the image of perfection".

A step to changing this belief is to recognize that we are the one observing the "self" image meaning that what we create is really non-self-imagery. With this awareness we can then decide to believe in the non-self-image or not. Having this awareness may help shift our point of view and is the initial step toward changing our beliefs.

You may be convinced that being hard on yourself will make you a better person or that you deserve to feel bad about who you are, but remember that those are just thoughts too and there is no guarantee that any thought you have is based on wisdom. Rather than struggling with low self-esteem, spend your energy learning how to stop buying into it and see if you can bring more self-compassion to your life.

You may start by implementing new actions and habits such as art and Yoga. This can open up a whole new world, filled with countless opportunities and possibilities. Yoga helps you gain more clarity by channeling your energy in a positive direction. The meditation techniques used in Yoga helps you to watch your thoughts. Although your thinking and self-perception will never be 100 percent positive, you must learn to dismiss negative thoughts and stay open to other ideas that will help you to move in a positive direction. This may be achieved by practicing to recognize negative thoughts quickly and using your mind to quell them immediately.

Yoga has many great advantageswith helping individuals deal with disappointment in a positive manner. Even the most successful people have to deal with disappointment, learn how to move to the next level of your life by processing your feelings and taking intentional actions toward bettering them.

With art you may also learn to trust yourself and your feelings again. You will discover the belief in your inner resources and your ability to rely on them, and that no matter what, you'll grow from those experiences. I believe that the answers usually lie within each and every individual, and without a doubt in my mind you are more than smart enough to figure out what you really need to do.

In a creative project, you also learn not to get so caught up in vain desires. Desire can be a powerful motivational tool, but wanting something too much can end up resulting in you paying a very painful and expensive price, oftentimes which you can't actually afford. This is not to say that you shouldn't dream big or chase the things your mind can barely fathom; but proper planning and preparation is essential, don't just throw all you've got on something you dreamt about last night; haste makes for great waste. Seek your desires, but keep your integrity.

Yoga – The mind movie

"We are what we think. All that we are arises with our thoughts. With our thoughts, we make the world." - Buddha

When we have an important meeting or want to accomplish an important task, like holding a presentation,we need to garner our self-esteem on a high level so that we can be our best selves. Regardless of what is taking place in life, we have the opportunity, through Yoga, to become centered in our feelings so that we can be rooted and grounded no matter what may come. While practicing Yoga, you learn to watch your thoughts as a silent detached witness. You create space between you and your thoughts.

A friend of mine had a presentation to give in front of one hundred people. I was happy to be in the audience because she had spectacular content and the ability to deliver well. Once she started to present, she commanded the attention of the audience and they listened to every single word that came out of her mouth! I met her after the presentation and congratulated her. She gave me only a mild smile. I asked her what was wrong. She told me that her mother was sick and had gone to the hospital last night. I expressed my sympathy and told her that she did so well nobody had even the slightest idea that something was wrong. She explained that she decided this morning that she had to options 1) get in her "head movie" and ponder how bad everything was or 2) find a calm space in her mind."So I decided for the calm space," she said.

In the west, we often associate Yoga with the Asana (Yoga poses) only. But Yoga is much, much more than just the poses. There many ancient Yoga philosophies and in one of them, the Yoga Sutras by Patanalij, Yoga is explained as the following: Yoga is restraining the activities of the mind. We often fail to conquer a task, not because of our abilities, but because of our mindset and preconceived ideas. One time, in the Ashram, we did a long meditation before the Asana class. So when we started the mind was calm and clear. We had to do some quite challenging Asanas and one I really struggled with before it worked all of a sudden. Simply because I was not caught in my head with ideasabout why I couldn't do it like: what if I fall, I never could do it before why should it work today, oh my neighbor is really good, I hope nobody sees that I cannot do it. No.This time my energy was focused. When I told my teacher afterwards he said,"where the mind goes, energy goes."

When I mentioned meditation to my students, they all have the same look on their face and I had that look too a decade back when it was suggested that I should start. Why is meditation scary for most of us?

1. First of all we have to sit still in a pose we never sit in. Not comfortable....
2. There is nothing around us no phone, no music, no laptops, no food. That's a state we seldom experience in our daily life.We sit with ourselves.
3. And then there is either this scary stillness or the many thoughts in our head. Both can become really, really loud; loud stillness loud thoughts.

So why spend time there? Simply because behind all this there is joy, peace and an immense power which we can use.

We cannot sit down and expect that meditation just happens and that we will bliss out in a second. But sitting with our thoughts and watching them in a detached way can be transferred in our daily lives. It improves the decisions we make, and our relationships when we are having a split second to observe the thoughts, and evaluate them before we react immediately to them.

You will learn different sitting poses, and, I promise, there is one for you. You will also learn some poses you can do before meditation so that sitting becomes easier. Those simple movements of your body will change the movements of your mind, therefore changing your motions can actually change your emotions. Then it's easier to sit. There are many ways to meditate and one is for you. Meditation on

sounds, guided meditation. Meditation on the
breath.

Meditation, even for just a few minutes, can lift your
spirit, and you can experience the peace that comes
when you are able to remove yourself from your
normal patterns of thought. You can discover that
our general state of being may not be the final
version of ourselves. In the end, we are something
more than our thoughts.

Exercise:

How to sit?

Most important is that you sit straight, whether it is
on the floor, on a chair or on a cushion. Sitting
straight helps you to sit in awareness during your
meditation. Also important is that your knees are
lower than your hips. Therefore it is recommend to
fold a blanket under your buttocks or to use a
cushion. If possible, try not lean against a wall or the
back of the chair.

Before you start:

Make sure you have a quiet, comfortable place for
your meditation in which you feel safe, and able to
close your eyes. Set a fixed time aside like 5, 10 or 15
minutes. If you feel restless, or have a lot going on in
your head that will make it hard to settle down,
make the following Asanas before you begin.

Cat/Cow to loosen the spine
Downdog to get a good stretch of your legs and
upper body
Seated forward bend to calm the mind
Eye Exercise to draw your senses slowly inward

Have something to write next to you. Then take a
comfortable seated position of your choice.Before
you start gentle but determinate ask your mind to be
quiet for the X minutes you have set aside. Like this:
I ask my mind to be quiet for the next 10 minutes. If
it does disagree, which is most likely, tell your mind:
"Next to me lies a notebook. I will take 5 minutes
time after my meditation and will write down all the
tasks and sorrows that you have and take care of
them. I promise."

Now become aware of the sounds around you. Hear
the sounds that are most distant without naming
them. Focus now on the thoughts that are closer to
you, also without labeling them. Then start to draw
your attention closer and into your body. Hear your
breathing. Inhaling, Exhaling, Inhaling, Exhaling.....
Whenever a thought arises watch it going by like a
distant cloud in the sky. The thought comes, the
thought goes. If you start to interfere with your
thoughts come back to the sound of your breath,
inhaling, exhaling. Sometimes it is useful to simply
identify the thought like: worry, anger, sorrow,
judging, blaming, planning....Focus on your breath.
In case you need more distance from the thoughts.
Imagine this: Your mind is like the ocean and deep

in the ocean it is calm and serene. You can watch your thoughts, your thought waves from deep down in the ocean on the surface as they appear. The waves come and go.

By creating a place in your mind where you simply observe your thoughts, you create space to which you can return whenever necessary.

Start with 5 minutes, it is useful to set a timer so that you are not wondering how long you have spent sitting there.

In whatever state of mind you started, I guarantee that even after a couple of minutes sitting and watching your breath you are able to break the thinking pattern you had before you started. With a little bit of practice you will be able identify negative thoughts without getting consumed by them.

Art - The letter and the portrait

"I do not paint a portrait to look like the subject, rather does the person grow to look like his portrait." - Salvador Dali

Every day we are bombarded with so many ideas about who we should be, and the ways we are expected to look and act that we often lose sight of who we truly are. We all struggle with self-acceptance every once in a while, and need someone or something to remind us of how awesome, talented and truly fortunate we are.Art can be the path which will help us to be more compassionate with ourselves, and ultimately with others. Art has a great way of tapping into our true, authentic selves; connecting our inward spirit with the opportunity of becoming outstanding by working on our self-esteem, self-worth, confidence and happiness.

One of my clients had to put on an Inner Self Mask vs. Outer Self Mask to survive in his job. Here, the inner self is who you are when you are alone and the outer self is how you make yourself appear to other people in different situations. When he came to me he was split into two personalities; the 'Inner Self' and the 'Outer Self' as he called it. We took our time to analyze the characteristics of each of these personalities and what types of emotions they experienced. Once this was completed, we work with what we found in a creative manner to visually represent both personalities. During this process magnificent works of art were created and a great exhibition developed from it.

The focus on introspective thinking is greatly beneficial to us all. It is for us to identify that which we want to make public, and those things which we want to remain private. This introspective declaration for the unveiling of these choices or decisions can lead to a further exploration of self and even to uncover the potential which we sometimes hide because of lack of awareness that we possess them.

Once he could identify these potentials, he had the option of turning them into affirmations. These affirmations help to develop a more positive self-esteem, and enhances the chances of becoming even more outstanding. Having a positive outlook about yourself can potentially re-wire the connections in your brain causing you to feel more confident about yourself. If we change negative thoughts into positive ones, our behaviors will likely follow!

Out of internet and magazines, I took some time to jot down the things that I would like for myself in the future. I took a look at where I was now and recognized things I would love to maintain for the future and things that I would love to change. Once I placed myself in this mindset of focusing on future goals, I started to see opportunities in magazines and select images/words that represent my goals. With this I developed specific goals. I became creative and abstained from trying to understand in that moment why that particular image or word spoke to me. Out of this I began to create my vision board.

You may consider this to be simple or even to petty to have any actual effect. However, it helped me to get comfortable looking at how I see the world and my own reflection. I more confidently practiced the act of not judging, but played with ideas, to help alleviate some of the critical thoughts I had about myself when I saw all that was taking place in the world. This exercise for me was more about looking at the world; as a set of ideas, shapes, lines, and colors and hopefully appreciating the opportunities and beauty of it instead of immediately finding the flaws. The Vision Board will give you the opportunity to have a different perspective and to cultivate the ability to become your most outstanding self.

For many people, expecting something special from life is undoubtedly stressful. Art can just be the simple act of taking time to focus on what you want out of life, and because it is just imagination it can help relieve some stress. It may also help you to focus on what you really want and what you need, and even provide the empowerment to achieve it!

STEPS:

- Write a love letter to yourself depicting what you love and appreciate about you. Make sure to be intimate, gentle and detailed; your aim is to look back in retrospect and see that you are valuable and worthy of great things!
- Now you will need to transform these symbols into an abstract Self-Portrait. You will need a canvas, paint brushes, paint, a palette or paper plates, water, paper towels, pencil and mirror.
- Find a comfortable place to sit. You can do this free or make sure you have a mirror in front of you so that you can see your face. Begin by outlining your head on the canvas with a pencil. This does not mean to be exact. This is about spending time with yourself,

learning the beauty of you and the experience of playing with art materials.

- Spend some time to identify which part of you face could represent what affirmation or symbol the best. For example: 'I believe in myself, like a rock' as my forehead, now you have a stone as your forehead. Once you have completed your project, again, do not judge!

Fighting your inner critic is one of the hardest parts about this specific task! Spend time writing down what the experience was like for you and what you see when you look at the portrait. The more abstract you work the more you will accept this work of art.

We spend so much of our day thinking about what we did wrong or why we're not good enough, without thinking about how much we have to offer this world. Give yourself credit for being incredible! By developing this art, you will feel compassion and love for yourself.

Allowing yourself to play with this self-image will hopefully connect you to the inner potentials we all have within us. Think about when you were young and were free to imagine and create in childhood.

There was definitely something carefree about that time, and a good reason for that is because we didn't judge ourselves! Giving ourselves the gift of tapping into that inner potential can truly open us up to a world possibilities where we can feel more comfortable with who we because we will find where we belong.

Chapter 3–A real treat

Intro – The opposite of work

We are all well aware of the fact that as much as hardwork is necessary to the realization of success, this hard work should be balanced with play for the purpose of rejuvenation and release. Oftentimes, it is quite evident that we neglect play, and place all our time and effort into work, thinking that it is a worthy sacrifice which may even make us more successful. Unfortunately, this notion is dead wrong! Play is just as important as work and we need to start making a conscious decision to start treating ourselves the way we deserve to be treated!

If someone told you to drop everything and go play right now, would you listen or would your other obligations keep you from leaving your desk? Our society has the bad habit of tying self-worth to inefficient productivity. As a result, we end up sacrificing treats like rest, being creative and our general health and even well-being if those things will get in the way of our work. When was the last time you told yourself to stay up for just one more hour to get more work done, despite the fact that you can barely keep your eyes open? Individuals see work and being creative as polar opposites. They think that by elimination one requirement for success, they can maximize on the other and reap the same or similar benefit. The opposite of creativity, health and feeling alive is not work but actually depression, so there really is no way to actually win in the end.

According to a research, "humans are biologically programmed to engage in purposeless activities that on the first sight might appearunproductive. To deprive ourselves of this treat of feeling alive is to do ourselves a great disservice." Don't be moved by the constant thought that treating yourself will make you lazy.In fact, cranking up treats can actually make you more productive by bringing back excitement and novelty to your job, whilst fostering empathy and creativity. Oftentimes, the things that we discover about ourselves during the treats are important to our success. It gives us time to identify our own set of gifts and talents that we can share with the world. How many times in our lives were we encouraged to deny ourselves of things which we are drawn to, and feel on top of the world when we do them? How often were we ask to quit spending all your time drawing, singing or playing and go do some math and science instead! It's high time you ignore this advice! We all have unique gifts and talents that belong to us alone, they were gifted to us for our use, to become better individuals and contributors to this amazing universe where we alone can fulfill the task on which our very existence lies. Rather than losing who you are to the demands and requirements of society, step out boldly and assume your place, the rewards may blow you out of this world!

Personal Development–Changing perspective

"Whatever liberates our spirit without giving us mastery over ourselves is destructive. And whatever liberates our spirit while giving us mastery over ourselves is constructive" - Goethe

In a way we all know that perfectionism is somewhat of a hindrance to growing into your future. It is an obsessive and debilitating loop whose cycle is never-ending closed system, with each cycle increasing in intensity. Don't get caught in the world-wind of this tiring and deceptive façade. Make it a point of duty to do your best and rest in the knowledge that your best is good enough, once it truly is your best!

It has been recognized that treats may be used to strengthen good habits! Yes, treats, like actually taking yourself out for dinner to that restaurant you have been wanting to visit for quite some time now, or even planning to go on a cross country excursion, not to mention those expensive shoes that happen to stare at you, screaming "buy me!" every time you pass your favorite store. Many popular treats come at a cost and can be demanding so it is also important to have some options that aren't very demanding; perhaps you may start with something smaller. A student once told me, "Every day after a meeting, I spend 10 minutes at the park, and enjoy looking at the trees, although I'm still at work, that little indulgence makes me very happy!

Another client thought she should renounce her treat of her favorite drink, and nope it's not water, it's actually champagne! "I really love champagne, but I know I should stop drinking it," she told me. "Why?" I expressed. "Does it make you drunk or dizzy? Does it make your stomach hurt?" She replied "No, it doesn't affect me. I told her that, you need some treats, and as treats go, champagne is great. Even if you buy very expensive champagne, it's not that expensive, in absolute terms. It relaxes you and can boosts your energy and focus. A treat or a habit isn't bad unless it causes some kind of problem."

We need to do some good to ourselves. When I get all down on myself, feel out of shape, or hear the ranting of the sometimes crazy person inside of me, there two things I tell to myself:

1. **You Are One of a Kind**

Every single one of us is unique in our own way. We all have special gifts and talents. You may have a head for math, an inquisitive mind, a talent for art like me or even the patience of a saint, literally.
Whatever it is, you are uniquely created to perform that gift and only you can offer it to this world in the way that you are expertly gifted to do so. It's time to wake up and acknowledge that you have something to offer that no one else can, use this difference to your advantage!

2. **Love What You've Got**

We often compare ourselves with the gifts of others, not realizing how long and hard those individuals had to work to get to the stage they are currently at, by completely forgetting this, we quickly assume that if only we had their gift, we would be more successful than we are right now. Never disrespect the gift! Stop thinking negatively and maximize on what you have, your gift will make way for you, if only you find it and learn to use it.

There is a big myth that I must clarify.It is that a treat must be a reward.The truth of the matter is that a treat doesn't necessarily have to be a reward. A reward is mere gratification or justification for some action performed. Conversely, a treat is a small pleasure or indulgence which we give to ourselves just because we want to, we don't need to earn it!

"Treats" may sound like a self-indulgent, frivolous strategy, but they're not. Forming good habits can be draining but treats can play an important role. When we give ourselves treats, we feel energized, cared for and content within ourselves, which boosts our self-command which in turn helps us to maintain our healthy habits. Studies have shown that people who get a little treat, in the form of receiving a surprise gift or watching a funny video, gained self-control. It's a secret of adulthood that If I give more to myself, I can ask more from myself because self-regard isn't selfishness.

Here are a few simple techniques which can set you free from the bondage of perfectionism.

1. **Remove Yourself from the Competition**

    Don't make life any more difficult than it already is. Most perfectionists are extremely competitive because being perfect means being the best at, well, everything. So choose your friends and associates wisely. For example, some professional organizations and artistic groups can be extremely supportive while some are just horrendous! As a perfectionist, you don't need folks feeding you the very message you are trying to forget."You are nothing without success" or "if you don't get there, I will!'". Instead check how they make you feel about your creativity, when you are not feeling boosted, don't go back!

2. <u>Show your Weakness</u>

This is counter intuitive for most perfectionists, but I guarantee that you'll get good results if you try it.Thinking in retrospect, every time I showcased my vulnerability to onlookers, the response was phenomenal; it is reassuring to know that you are not alone in whatever you are struggling with.When you are real, art lovers don't recoil in disgust. They come closer.

3. <u>Add Some Color</u>

Perfectionists are color blind.They basically see the world in black and white. To open up your field of view to a wider perception, it is important to do away with the narrow-minded and one track mentality. Take off your blinkers by looking beyond the surface of things and circumstances which you encounter and you will discover a whole new world of thinking and being.

Challenge yourself by trying to reduce your inner perfectionist. This may be easier when we make a conscious effort to treat ourselves which may provide some rejuvenation, as opposed to feeling depleted, resentful and angry for lack of self-indulgence. When we become burdened by lack, it is general to grab anything we see at the first sign of what we may want because we are hungry for comfort! This may break habits which we have tried so desperately to maintain. So choose your treats mindfully.

Yoga – Moving into happiness

"Have no fear of perfection - you'll never reach it." - Salvador Dali

What I love about Yoga is that it is not competitive. When you ask in a class why the students do Yoga, you get the most different answers: Relaxation, fitness, spirituality, breathing, quiet mind, well-being. But what nearly all Yoga practitioners reportafter a Yoga class is that they feel whole. In Sanskirt, one of the words for perfection is "purna", which can be translated as fullness or wholeness. Indian yogi texts tell us that all in this world arises from and is contained inside one single energy. That one energy is in everything; in an untidy room, unfinished work, a beautiful Mozart symphony or in a sunrise. We are in touch with that energy all imperfections are revealed as part of the whole. We define perfect in our everyday life with flawless.

After one class,I talked with my students about the day's experiences. One student pointed out that she struggled hard in her headstand practice today. Her neighbor immediately commented in support of her saying, "I saw you upside down that was a perfect headstand; straight, steady, balanced." She replied that it might have looked that way but her mind was racing and it was hard for her to be in the present moment and relax. While we might be admiring the flexibility of a person next us the person tries to relax, and has not even the goal to become more flexible. Everybody is on their own journey and we never know which stage a person may be on in that journey. What looks good on the outside might not feel good on the inside. Every practice is entirely your own practice and this offers an immense freedom. If you are focused on comparing yourself to others, you are stealing the benefits that Yoga can bring from yourself.

When I started my practiceeight years ago, I was fixed on achieving the poses, and kept asking myself whether or not I did it better than my neighbor, or if I even did it right at all! Sooner or later, I came to recognize that I didn't actually become enlightened when I reached a pose. I also learned that there is no such thing as a final pose. It is an evolutionary development and it is simply in the nature of the human mind to strive to the next highest stage once we reached our goal.

Many perfect images have been planted in our heads. Social media portrays happiness and a grand life.We must remember in the midst of this that nearly nobody will show the struggles they are going through in the social arena, as it is the norm of society to pretend as though everything is perfect! There is no need to feel sorry for ourselves by comparing ourselves to what people choose to show, the truth lies behind the camera!And of course our definition of perfect

Keeping the focus inward can help you to own your practice. Where are my thoughts today? What does my body feel like? How is my breath flowing? These questions don't have to be answered.Their purpose is to give your mind something to focus on so you can eliminate distractions. The following poses are easy to access and very beneficial to your nervous system. Practicing these poses for yourself brings a great deal of happiness and balance into your life. This practice is your practice. Set an intention before you start with the poses, for example:"Today I will focus on my breathing, today I will focus on my movements."The intention remains an intention, and not a goal which has be to reached. With an intention, the practice will become your own and it will be a treat for you. These handful of poses might make you feel perfect even when they are not flawless.

Sequence:

Half Sun Salutations

1. Tadasana Mountain Pose hands in prayer

2. Inhale raise your hands and look at your thumbs
3. Exhale bend forwards, touch your thights, shines, or feet. Relase your neck. You can bend your knees.
4. Inhale lengthen your spine until it is parallel to the floor
5. Exhale bend forwards (as in 3)
6. Inhale rise to standing, arms up and look at your thumbs (as in 2).

Repeat for 5 times. Stand in Position on for a couple of breaths.

Uttanasana (Standing forward bend) / Utkatasana (Chair Pose)

Stand in a forward bend. With the inhale raise your arms and bend your knees come into Chair Pose. Repeat that movementa couple of times and hold each pose for two breaths.

With the last forward bend come onto all fours.

Marjaryasana / Bitilasana -Cat/Cow

Place your knees in line with your hips, and your hands in line with your shoulders. In the neutral position your spine is straight. Inhale and on the exhale draw your belly to your spine and round your back towards the ceiling into cat. On the inhale drop your belly towards the mat. Lift your chin and chest gaze up towards the ceiling. Repeat this movements fluently in the rhythm of your breath. Let breath and movement become one.

Supta Maatsyendrasana – Reclined Lord of the fish pose

Lie on the back. Bend the right leg and place the sole of the foot near your buttocks. Your left leg is straight. Place your left hand on the bend knee and take the right arm in out to your side in a T-shape. Inhale and on the exhale roll to your left side. So that your knee touches the ground. The head is on the left side. Breathe into your side body. Stay still and take a couple of deep breaths. Inhale and on the exhale come out and change sites.

Viparit Karani -Legs up the wall (or translated directly reversed action ;))

Move your mat with the short side to the wall. Sit sideways and move your buttocks close to the wall. Now lie on your back and have your legs supported from the wall. Place your hand on either side or place one hand on the heart and one hand on the belly. Stay here for a minute. With as little effort as possible go into Savasana

Savasana - Corpse pose

Lay on your back, spread your arms 45 degrees, palms are facing up, thumbs are near the floor so that your shoulders are on the ground. Your chin should be parallel to your chest.If your neck is uncomfortable, place a thin blanket or towel under your head. Your legs are hip width apart and your feet are falling loosely outward. If your lower back feels compressed, place a pillow under your knees. Stay in this position for at least 5 minutes. To come out, roll on your right side and bend your knees (fetus position), remain here for some breath. Support yourself with your right hand to sit up.

Stay seated for a couple of minutes and enjoy the feeling.

Art – Zen Madala a pattern of beauty

"Find beauty not only in the thing itself but in the pattern of the shadows, the light and dark which that thing provides." - Junichiro Tanizaki

Very often we come down extremely hard on ourselves because we do not match up with the idea of perfection enshrined in our heads. It is as though we lack any respect and appreciation for the talents we have, although they might be a bit rough around the edges. Think of it this way, if you think you suck at the piano and don't fit in with the musical geniuses with whom you are affiliated, first be thankful for the gift of hands which are used to manipulate this instrument to bring about spectacular sounds. We tend to get so caught up in the notion of idealism in our heads that we take even the most necessary and vital implements to our success for granted because they are always readily available. If you need some motivation, consider if a friend was in your position and not doing as well as they desired, would you yell and scream at that person and tell them that they are no good? Exactly! The same is required of you! Motivate yourself!

Embrace your art and potential by indulging in your gifts, you may uncover something new every time you try.

Pleasure and art is what I experience on a daily basis, not only in my art, but also from my students. There have been very significant advances in our understanding of what happens in our brains when we look at works of art. Recently, science has discovered that when we look at things we consider to be beautiful, there is increased activity in the pleasure reward centers of the brain. There is a great deal of dopamine in this area, also known as the 'feel-good' transmitter. Essentially, this is where the smiles of my students are birthed from after an art session.

During my work with managers, I have found that a self-compassionate attitude that allows you to treat yourself has increased the student's creativity and productivity, especially those who are chronically self-judgmental. I have found that individuals with high self-judgmental attitudes have benefited from a self-compassionate mindset, as they consequently produced significantly more original answers than their less self-judgmental counterparts.

To achieve such a self-compassionate mindset I started to helpthe studentsto develop their confidence. When students experience pleasure in art, they do it over and over and over again, and after a time they become great at it; being good at something gives you confidence, and in return you experience great pleasure.

A great path which I used for my studentsto find confidence and take pride in themselves was helping them develop their mindset. In today's culture, society boasts accolades such as awards and rewards. However, if you are able to take pride in yourself and cultivate appreciation for those things which you are able to do, your confidence might take you places that skill alone probably wouldn't.

I have learned that when you endure a challenge in life, you need to have a strong team around you. Whether you are fighting to keep your company afloat, facing an illness in the family, or you just lost your job, your mental strength is more likely to come from those whom you are surrounded by. To understand that you can only give to others what you have generated in yourself was also a lesson for me. If you keep giving to others and the stores of your kindness aren't being restored, sooner or later you will end up empty with no one to refill you. Additionally, it took me some exercises of mental toughness to convince myself to let pleasure happen in my life so that I may share it with others.

It is still a myth that being good to yourself is not right. This may seem strange but for most people it would be okay to grab your iPod or your notepad and draw up a list of all the things that are negative, but to write things you can do today to make yourself feel good prove somewhat of a challenge. We all know that small pleasures like laughing, practicing Yoga or even a long leisurely dinner with friends can do us a lot of good.Stop holding back on living life, and throw your all at the things your heart longs for.Just do them.

One of my main rules is that if something negative happens, you must laugh. Accept that you are indeed the source of many wonderful things and keep remembering them from time to time. A student told me after she returned from my art retreat that she wanted to live her life every day as if she was still on the retreat.

With time I have developed many "feel good" and pleasurable art methods. One of them is Zen-Mandala. This is the process of pleasurable drawing or painting, with the actual term being quite similar to the meditative state taught in the art of Zen. This is basically a system which allows almost anyone to relax and express themselves in a creative way, while enjoying the beauty of simple pleasures.

The system follows certain steps, which are established to create freedom within the boundaries. These are:

1. Zen-Mandala s are drawn within a circle.
2. From the center lines dividing the circle, there are official tangles, it's most pleasurable if they have a symmetry. While this may sound overly constraining, it is actually meant to create more relaxation without a lot of thinking.
3. In this boundaries and sections we start to create the patterns. This patterns follow no rules and are drawn very lightly with a pencil.
4. Next we will fill this pattern with color or black and white. It is a highly-focused process designed to facilitate relaxation.
5. The only rule is that youstay in flow and relax, while not making it a stressful process. While these sound like work, there is really no wrong way. While the end result may actually turn out to be lovely; it's really about the process.

Studies have further shown that art may actually help you to pay greater attention to other things going on around you. So doing small creative art works during a lecture or a meeting, though everyone else thinks you are being rude and not listening, will actually help your mind focus on what is being said.

Zen-Mandala is easy-to-learn, relaxing and it is fun to create beautiful images by drawing structured patterns, the great part is that almost anyone can do it! It further increases focus and creativity, provides artistic satisfaction along with an increased sense of personal wellbeing.

All you need is to perform exercises which will strengthen your mental toughness, and this is more than worth it. So next time you catch yourself dismissing your ideas or creative attempts as not good enough, think whether you would have the same response to a friend. If the answer is no, simply think about how you would treat a friend in a similar situation, and apply that attitude towards your own creative endeavors. By challenging yourself with a skill you are not fully mastering, you develop greater confidence in your skills and creativity and avoid meltdowns when the latter failures to occur. It is bound to help you tap into your enormous wealth of creative potential.

Chapter 4 Shaping success

Intro – Embrace your intuition

In today's world, we are constantly bombarded by the portrayal that, in order to lead a fulfilling life, we must be good at making decisions and trusting our own intuition. As a matter of fact, being in tune with one's intuition is one of the greatest assets you can have for leading the life you have always dreamt of. Many people generally mistake intuition as just being a "gut feeling", but the truth is, it may physically reveal itself as a gut feeling but it is way more than just that. In reality, intuition and reason are directly proportional to each other; and when your brain makes a particular observation, it searches through your catalogue of memories in order to find relevant information. This relevant information is then compiled into the "gut feeling" that sends you in a flow of right actions.

It is this exact process of unconsciously drawing on previous experiences that allows athletes like basketball players for example, to know the precise angle and force they need to shoot a three-pointer without having to sit down first to do the math. So, we can't just think of intuition as the opposite of reason. Rather, intuition is simply a way of reasoning that leaves room for uncertainty when making decisions. By embracing your intuition, you put trust in both yourself and prior experiences that have contributed to the shaping of your knowledge on each subject. This enables you to remain confident based on your previous knowledge, despite not knowing exactly how the situation at hand will be diffused. The basketball player, for example, can't be certain that the ball will swish through the hoop, but he can make an educated guess based on his intuition.

On the other hand, not everyone is confident enough to pursue challenges despite risk and uncertainty, this may result in them being overly emotional when faced with simple tasks that just require a tad bit of reasoning. However, this is not a skill that is developed overnight. With each risk comes a new and possibly higher level of required trust in yourself and confidence in your experiences. Just think about it this way, the challenges which you face are just a barrier between where you are and the things you wish to achieve.
Instead of being fearful and cowering away when faced with the undesirable, simply approach the issue with gratitude and thankfulness, as when you overcome it, you will be advancing to a higher level which will ultimately make the life you envision a reality!

Personal Development –Ask and receive

"The important thing is not to stop questioning; curiosity has it's ow reason for existing." – Albert Einstein

The questions you're regularly exposed to act as guidelines that have the ability to powerfully influence your direction and the success of your life. Undoubtedly, the questions which you tend to hear often come from inside of you, and this is for good reason! However, when looking to answer these questions, we generally seek to find validation from outside sources, not realizing that we have ability to both ask and answer the questions that tend to consume our minds; this is where the development of self-awareness begins.

Being one of the primary practices which develop self-awareness, Yoga is an infinitely rich guide on how to spend the hours you are not on the mat! Awareness is a connection that occurs in the deep parts of your brain, it is a deep level of understanding not just of one's self but of one's surroundings. It brings a sense of togetherness with the many parts of the mind, however, it's not always easy to access the heightened awareness you find during Yoga. One of strengthening this connection is to become more aware of how the small choices you make every day affect you, your community, and the world around you.

Maybe this year you'd like to take better care of your body, help others, or increase your impact. If you are not true to yourself and deny aspects of who you are, you are not going to experience things the way you were meant to, or the way that would be the most beneficial to your development.

Oftentimes, I come into contact with students and clients who really desire to do all the right things, their biggest problem is that they engage in the exact opposite of what they are attempting to achieve. They hope to experience growth in certain areas of their lives, but they resist change- which is the only catalyst which can turn their situation around. They want to lead a less stressful life, yet they continuously associate themselves with people and things that induce drama. They long for better relationships, but they sit around sulking day in and day out that they have no one. Simply put, what they say and what they do are constantly in opposition and are hopelessly disconnected. Without intentional intervention, the situation is more or less hopeless!

I myself needed some confidence and courage for my first steps to rituals of success.

In the beginning of my art career, it was very hard for me to create a piece of art and enter it into an art exhibit. My guess wasthat most of the artists or creative individualscan't enter their pieces successfully on the first, so I made up lots of stories and excuses in my head like; you have "no talent, time, tools, techniques and so on". However, the questions I now ask myself are: what kind of quality questions do I have to ask myself to get rid of the stories that are holding me back? What kind of ritual do I have to develop to become successful?

In the beginning it was most definitely difficult to say the least, but with time, persistence and hard work; I have learnt to develop successful systems which allow me to reap extremely beneficial rewards!

Getting out of your comfort zone and relentlessly pursuing your most cherished dreams isn't to be taken lightly, as it is most definitely not a simple stroll in the park! Change is extremely hard to deal with, but there comes a time when you must weight where you are with where you want to go and determine whether or not it is worth pushing past what you already have in life! Old habits are very hard to break, but are you comfortable with just dreaming for the rest of your life? Or do you actually want to do something about it?

Another truth which we must face is that we often waste too much time in fruitless places! We spend a lot of time on Facebook, watching our favorite reality television shows, on the phone chatting with friends and engaging in other time consuming activities that will hinder our progression. Instead, try to use most of the time used on these activities to free your mind so that you can think more openly and embrace your inner creativity, as opposed to being confined by the things which you see and hear.

Isn't it funny how we easily get accustomed unhealthy rituals? Day by day nothing changes, but when we reflect in retrospect, we come to the realization of how far we have journeyed from the hindrances of temporary comfort. That's the power of daily rituals!

If you are honest with yourself and ask quality questions you will become aware of your unhealthy rituals. Here are some rituals for long-term happiness and success that have been successful in my work with students and clients.

1. <u>**Choose Who and What You Give Yourself To**</u>

Ralph Emerson once said "The only person you are destined to become is the person you decide to be." So make new choices as needed, rather than letting old ones make you. In this life, you don't choose if you get hurt, but you have the capacity to choose who and what could possibly hurt you! After all, who we ultimately become depends, in part, on who and what we let into our lives. So don't just settle for relationships and situations that have proven to be unworthy. Exercise your right to choose differently.

Be the hero of your own life and stop playing the victim. You may not be able to control all the circumstances that happen to you, but you can decide not to be continuously reduced by the same ones.

2. Loosen your Grip on What's not Meant for You

Things will happen that you will not always be able to understand, but maybe you're not supposed to understand everything, maybe you're just supposed to have faith, accept it and let go of your worries. Positive things happen in your life when you emotionally distance yourself from the negative things. So stop holding on to what hurts, and make room for what feels right. Don't let what is out of your control interfere with all the things you can control.

3. Steer Clear of Drama and Those who Create it

There comes a time in life when you have to let go of all the needless drama and the people who create it. Staying out of other people's drama is an incredibly effective way to stress less and smile more.

4. Be positive and Spend Time with Positive People

Happiness is not the absence of problems, but the ability to deal with them. Raise your awareness and inner strength to embrace positive outcomes. You are in charge of how you react to the people and events in your life. You can either give negativity power over your life, or you can choose to be positive by focusing on the great things that are truly important. So, talk about your blessings more than you talk about your problems. Just because you're struggling doesn't mean you're failing. Every great success requires some kind of worthy struggle to get there.

5. Ask Yourself the Right Questions

I think it was Voltaire who once said, "Judge a man by his questions rather than by his answers." This is such sound advice, because if you keep asking yourself the wrong questions, you will never get the answer you deserve. So, what questions are you asking yourself? Are they helping you better understand your purpose? Or do they have your mind spinning in circles?

In a nutshell, when it comes to working hard to achieve a substantial life goal of any kind, like earning a degree, building your career, painting, doing Yoga, becoming more mindful, or any other personal achievement that takes time and commitment; one thing you have to ask yourself is, "Am I willing to spend a little time every day like many people won't, so I can spend the better part of my life like many people can't?"

Think about it. We ultimately become what we repeatedly do. The acquisition of knowledge doesn't mean you're growing; growing happens when what you change the way you live.

Yoga- Worshipping the sun

"Turn your face towards the sun and the shadows fall behind you."

If you make the sun salutations your daily ritual you have the opportunity to have a
quiet mind, feelings of rest and joy with only little of time and even without leaving the house. It's an energetic sequence designed to make you strong, powerful, glowing and confident. The sun salute enables you to enter a flowing jet meditative state with little effort. The sun salutation is usually practiced in the morning and is a wonderful way to awaken the whole body.

A former colleague of mine was not what we would call a morning person. She often came in after 9 a.m. tired and fatigued with a croissant in her right hand and a cup of coffee in her left hand. She locked herself in her office, and after 10 a.m. she was the person we loved and admired; energized, happy and in full working mode. During the offered office Yoga class, she learned the sun salutation and as a new year's resolution, she decided to practice it every morning after she stood up. The office staff started to make bets.The jackpot was quite high. After a couple of weeks she stood energized in the office at 8 a.m. She smiled, talked to everybody and left her office door open. In a way she was carrying the sun in her whole body. Her light shone from within. The sun salutation not only changed how she inhibited her body, but her morning rituals. Instead of grabbing a coffee and croissant on the way she had a breakfast at home and her nice cup of coffee relaxed in the office.

After my first Yoga vacation in India, I asked my Yoga teacher how often I should practice Yoga. He said why don't you practice every day like you did here. I had a thousand reasons why I couldn't; no time, no studio, no group, no teacher, work, and household and so on. But after I came home from the vacation, funnily enough, my body woke me in the morning when I usually practiced. I found myself stretching in bed even before I woke up. My body demanded it, I started to practice every morning not a full class but what I could time wise and bodily wise. Yogasnuck into my life.

We often think we have to do a lot to get healthier and more vibrant. A membership in a sport studio, fancy sport clothes, friends or colleagues to join. The good thing about Yogais that you need only three things: yourself, a mat and comfy cloths. As my Yoga teacher once said: There was a time when we practiced Yoga without mats and without lulu lemon clothes. Yoga can be practiced nearly everywhere: in a studio, at home, in hotel room or open air. Where your mat fits is your space for Yoga.

I will break down the sun salutation, and show you different variations. Whatever your physical state might be the sun salutation is adjustable. Sun salutes can start on a chair and end with floating handstands in between. Most important is the synchronization of breath and movement.

With a little bit of practice the movement, breath and mind will become one.

It is important to start slowly. You want to practice today so that you will be able to practice tomorrow.

Art -Starting to flow

"The painting has a life of its own. I try to let it come through." - Jackson Pollock

Life itself trains us for success, and the only thing that can keep us away from achieving what lies in wait is ourselves. It is quite often suggested that self-worth and artistic success are equally yoked because of the nature of the work.If you think of art as a job, then your product is so much more than hours invested. The product is a piece of yourself, so of course if the reception is not the greatest, it may cause you to feel as though you are what people perceive about your work; let's just say that it is pretty intimate. Sometimes we get the feeling that if we don't build our success brick by brick without failing, we will neveramount to our greatestaspirations, but this is all just a lie that the negative committee in your head tells you for fear that they will no longer have a place to live, sooner or later. The trick to developing a ritual for success is to close the gap between you and your work, become so intimate and expressive through your work that others will be able to feel you just by viewing it!Once transferred from art into your career it is an opportunity to keep building your success more independently.

When I asked my students to contrast success with the state of a creative block, most of them described being in a trance-like ritual, which is what psychologists refer to as a "flow". Just by working steadily, every student can develop a state of flow, total clarity and nothing but great ideas will bubble up in their heads. For most of them it's like they are on top of the world and work seems to be just pouring out of them. This is what I call a ritual of success. This is most definitely possible when you put so much of yourself and your time into something; it becomeshard to separate it from who you are because you become it and it becomes you!

When I started my art career after the academy, I got stuck pretty often. However, I subsequently realized that by searching for things that would provide some form of excitement, I could get myself back on track. Also, I find this a bit humorous, but it is the times when I monkey around, more than doing actual and technical work that I find myself to be most successful. If you're struggling a bit, just try relaxing!

Stop being so hard on yourself.Always remember that you can never be finished creating art, it is a continuous process filled with lots of exploration and experimentation. It is a never ending journey with innumerable things to explore, and each and every success or failure places you right where you need to be so that you can get up again and chase your destiny. Don't shy away from the developmental stages, just go with the flow! So for now, take what you can from criticism and let go of the rest; accept what is and be grateful for what is to come. I guarantee you, it won't always be what you want to hear, but that is often exactly what is needed. It can be very confronting, but very useful.

There is no right way to be successful at art. So in reality, there isn't really a clear road to success which is suitable for everyone! It is for each of us to recognize who we really are and grow into who we are called to be. Success will not look the same for everyone, so stop comparing yourself to the accomplishments of others and planning your steps accordingly, as someone once said, "do you boo!". If today you wake up and feel like painting by throwing a large canvas on the floor of your studio and spilling dollops of paint all over it then sliding through the paint, thus spreading it all over the canvas. I have only three words: go do it!

The easiest way to develop a ritual for success is to engage in the things that you love! Find something that relaxes you and allows you to connect with who you are and what you stand for on a deeper level and use these places or events to activate your inner flow. You might be surprised at how beneficial it may even be to sit in a quiet room and just meditate, sooner or later you will get whisked away on the flow of a lifetime while you come face to face with amazing ideas and your greatest desires! There is not set framework for accomplishing this, the most valuable information which I can give to you is to relax and be led by your spirit to fulfilling what you are drawn to.

Tip: If you can't get into this mood there is an exercise that woks with patience. Choose one thing you love to draw or paint (and feel comfortable drawing or painting) already: an animal, object, a person, whatever. For thirty days, draw or paint that thing thirty different ways, a different way every day. You can use different mediums, expressions, positions, colors, whatever. Each day, push yourself to do something much different than the day before, but keep the subject the same. See how keeping one element constant, in this case, the "thing" you love to draw or paint, can become a ritual that allows you to break out creatively in other ways and get into the flow.

In art, one of the most powerful mindsets is to stay in the productive flow of things. Take the time to invest yourself so deeply into your work that even if you are surrounded by innumerable distractions, you will have the resilience and focus to stay committed to the task at hand. You may also come to the realization that when you learn to master the ability to focus, you can then transfer these principles to other areas of your life which may cause you to observe drastic improvements.

One of the greatest opportunities for self-growth through art is by recognizing that the criticism which we subject ourselves to opens us up to learning things that may encompass the key to our success. In art we can learn how to turn a deaf ear to naysayers and focus on satisfying our own souls instead. Remember that you won't be able to please everyone who comes into contact with your work, but you can most definitely benefit from all forms of criticism to make yourself a better individual, and by extension artist!

Chapter 5 -Have fun!

Intro- Cultivating individuality

What often holds us back from enjoying life are the
things that we have not done and have to do.
Comparing ourselves to others is totally natural and
something that we all do. However, in our attempts
to measure ourselves against our peers, we often end
up actually ridding ourselves of the very qualities
that make us interesting individuals.
Indeed, comparison is the very root of conformity.
While competition and conformity might at first
sound like polar opposites, they're actually
inextricably related. Whenever we compete, we
necessarily compare ourselves to others by means of
very narrow criteria.Because of this, we won't bother
to compete with people from entirely different
traditions and backgrounds, yet get riled up about
the very people who live next door.
While we might not compare our homes to the
mansions across town, we're likely to compete over
who has the best kept lawn on the block. However,
because we only compete with those who are similar
to us already, we ensure that we will follow the path
of conformity.
If we want to transcend these arbitrary comparisons,
we must open up to our own possibilities by
embracing our own individuality. When we focus on
our own unique gifts, it reminds us that the world

consists of individuals, each of whom makes unique and incomparable contributions.

In order to let your individuality shine, you'll first need to cultivate your creativity and well-being. But what if you aren't creative or not feeling good right now to enjoy life?

There are no such things as being completely healthy or born creative but there is a clear distinction between those who make use of their life and creativity and those who don't, so don't get hung up on whether you're fit or creative enough; just get out there enjoy life and create and it doesn't matter if you paint, do Yoga, write, make music or whatever else. As long as you're creating, you're also cultivating your individuality.

What we can learn from artist and yogis is to embrace your own potential and just start to enjoy life, move and create.

How many of Picasso's paintings can you name? Two? or Three?

He actually painted over 1,000 works of art because that is the nature of artists; they produce!

Artists don't worry about having bad ideas that turn into failures, because they know that as long as they persistently still produce art, good ideas will be made. The fact that some failures are produced is just an inevitable cost of success.

At the last moment, before completing something, most people begin doubting themselves; asking themselves questions like "is this really ready?" or "is it good enough to show the world?" But this is when true artists step up and enjoy themselves.

Always remember that products must ship or they won't be bought. Stories must be printed or they won't be read. Even the best ideas are useless if they lack an audience.

Personal Development – Faux fun and real fun

"If it's not fun, you're not doing it right." – Bob Basso

Why do some of us put off the most creative, fantastic, mood-enhancing thing in our lives?

To open up and have fun is a perspective. It's not a force bound within rules.The world can also be a playground to success.

Some of my students from a hard career background had no idea of what they love doing. They never experienced real fun, and never foundwhat they enjoy. I tried to focus and help them in any way I could. This was a serious case for me.Sometimes I would demand they get a medical checkup because the problem may be exhaustion, illness, or chemical imbalance, in which case they would need treatment. If that isn't the issue, they might have unhealed emotional wounds, such as a trauma or loss they have never processed. Art and Yoga can help make a difference.

Some were developing a faux fun. A lady namedGabi gave up the faux fun of drinking too much.She discovered that her perpetual alcohol fun had masked a profound lack of joy in her perfect looking life. Her career could not stand the strain then overnight Gabi went from being a manager to a starving student. When she later enrolled in college,

she calls me often to say, "I have no money, but I've never had so much fun in my life! Today, Gabi is taking the board exams to get her PhD.
This isn't the sort of life that pops into our minds when we hear the phrase "girls just want to have fun," but I think maybe it should. Although most people don't stray as far from their purpose as Gabi did because we all tend to take unexpected and interesting turns when we do what thrills us most.

I am dead serious about fun. As a coach, I am determined to help all my students have as much fun as they possibly can. I'm often surprised by how vehemently some of them reject this idea. They see fun as trivial, unworthy, disreputable. Maybe they'll have fun and start to connect with others someday, they tell me, but not until they've made a huge fortune or a scientific breakthrough or an artistic masterpiece. What they don't realize is that people who achieve such things are the ones who have fun doing them and communicating a lot. Opening up and having fun is not a diversion from a successful life; it is rather the pathway to it.

My views on fun are rather a narrow definition of the word. Fun is sometimes used to describe both the best and worst of human behavior. Bullies may torment others for "fun"; addicts may have "fun" that destroys their health and relationships. Some things that we call fun in our sociality aren't really fun. They're faux fun, and they lead straight to misery. It isn't difficult to tell faux and real fun apart once

109

you've learned to recognize the manic giddiness of the former and the nourishing pleasure of the latter.

If you're not clear which is which, the following factors can help you spot a fake:

1. Faux fun helps you ignore problems; real fun helps you face them.

2. Faux fun gets boring; real fun never does. Real sources of fun are what psychologists call renewable pleasures; they are enjoyable no matter how many times you do them.

3. If you're having real fun, you'll never regret it.

4. You can identify them by their wretched aftermath i.e. the discomforts of alcohol abuse are obvious, but all faux fun creates a hangover; though instincts are telling you that at least part of the fun was false.

In a way it is easy to find real fun in small steps. These simple techniques can reconnect you with your sense of fun.

Technique 1: Fishing for smiles.
Sit down with a notebook and list things you enjoy, this could be anything from picking your teeth to touring Nepal. As you write down each item, seriously consider doing that very thing later in the day or theweek or the year. The Spontaneous Smile is a smile that bubbles up almost irrepressibly, like a

beach ball popping out of water. Smiling is relaxing. I've seen this happen to people, and felt it happen to me while contemplating very small pleasures; say, tickling a cat ;or very large ones i.e. getting married. I've learned to trust this response as a powerful clue from the true self, a signal that one's innate sense of fun has been awakened and is pointing the way to a joyful and meaningful life.

Technique 2: Childhood revisited.
Genetic research suggests that our fun preferences are largely inborn and remain consistent throughout life. The time when we're free to act on them is usually childhood, so that's another great place to look for your fun print.
In your trusty notebook, begin listing things you remember enjoying as a child. Pay particular attention to things that made you "lose time," so that hours seemed to disappear in seconds. What absorbed you completely? Telling stories? , Climbing trees? , Playing dress-up?
You may want to ask family members, whose recollections can jog your memory. The next step is to look for patterns in this childhood fun. Did you like playing alone or with others? Inside or outside? Calmly or roughly? With words, objects, or actions? Almost certainly those preferences still exist in you, even after all the years in prep school or prison or wherever, no socialization is so complete that it can override the fun print buried in our genes. Choosing careers, avocations, and personal activities that fit this code will make you happier and more purposeful across the board.

These ideas we are using to gain momentum. When we develop a taste for fun again it's easy to take the next steps. Here are some tips that connect us again with our child hood.

Use your imagination.
A child can get lost in her make-believe world for hours. Imagine riding an elephant in Thailand. Or running a marathon on the Great Wall of China. You'll have so much fun pretending that you might want to make it a reality which leads to more fun than you can ever imagine.

Get out of your comfort zone.
As kids we take risks all day long. As we mature, we tend to stay in our safe place. Your day will be so much more exciting if you gather the guts to do something different. First small steps but in time your confidence will grow.

Slow down.
Children know how to take their sweet time. Allow yourself enough time to enjoy living. Rushing sucks all the fun out of the day.

Move and Create.
Paint, draw, build and write. Kids clearly enjoy those activities. Fun is being in your creative element.

These are the first steps, and there are many opportunities to practice the right mindset.

Each of us is born with a propensity to have fun and exchange with others doing certain types of activities. In certain proportions, you may love doing something I hate and vice versa. The pattern of activities you enjoy most is called "fun print," and like your thumbprint it's unique. It seems obvious to that we are most productive, persistent, creative, and flexible when we're engaged in precisely the combination of activities that brings us maximum fun. Your fun print isn't a frivolous indulgence. It is the map of your true life, an instruction manual for your essential purpose, written in the language of joy. Learning to read and respond to it is one of the most crucial things you'll ever do, all you have to do is be where you are.

Kids are really good at enjoying the moment. Adults are addicted to thinking about all the things they have to do tonight, tomorrow, next week. Where you are is where the fun is.

If you want to start today, start perhaps with a journal of fun and the people you play with. This technique requires that you keep a cursory "fun and friends journal" on a calendar. Every day jot down a brief list of your major activities and the people you interact with. Give each experience a fun score, with zero meaning no fun and ten meaning great fun. As the days go by, you'll begin to see which activities or people gives the most fun then you'll be surprised. My clients almost always find that the activities they think will be supremely fun consistently rank lower than things they've been taking for granted. Almost all of us can have wonderful fun without much money, education, beauty, and power as we think we need.

We are born with a complete understanding of fun, which seems to fade over time. I say we learn a thing from children.

Yoga – Connect to the heart

The key purpose of this Yoga Classic is to encourage you to reach out and touch others, and in turn to allow yourself to be touched by the joys of life. It's a chance to open up your heart, metaphorically and spiritually. We all have felt light hearted and heavy hearted. We can feel our heart jump, stand still or beat quickly. Not only at a physical level but also on an emotional level. The chest and the heart center are an important center.

Emily, one of my fellow yogis, had a kind of aversion against backbends. She was physically fit and had a healthy spine. When we discussed this in our group she said she felt exposed. Our teacher explained that the Asanas worked physically and mentally and energetically. We were all encouraged to look deeper; and surprisingly, at the end of our course she did the backbends with more and more joy. During my office days I was a slave to my bad posture. I felt often compressed; closed up and anxious. With Yoga, I was able to improve the flexibility of my upper back and open up my chest. I could transfer my Asana Body feeling in my office chair and I improved rapidly.Activities such as driving, working at the computer, eating, writing, and habitual posture and the effect of gravity can cause an exaggerated kyphotic curve with rounded shoulders. When the body is continually in this shape, the heart and lungs tend to be compressed.

When we open that specific area we are able to breathe properly and feel uplifted. There is no magic behind it, it is just a mindful asana practice focused on this neglected area. We will warm up with sun salutations and then do a series of backbends to open up the chest. Backbends will make you feel energized and joyful. I will guide you through some sun salutes and preparation poses and then we will dive in the heart center.

Art –Tap in your creative force

All children are artists. The problem is how to remain an artist once we grow up. - Pablo Picasso

With art it's easy to open up and tap into your inner wisdom and get those creative juices flowing. Having trouble tapping into your intuition? Make something! Snap some photos, Move freely, play music or you start to paint. It doesn't matter what the medium is, as long as it is done in the spirit of freedom and spontaneity.Sometimes referred to as intuitive art, this type of spontaneous expression helps you connect to the deeper parts of yourself, others and the realm of intuition, inspiration, and infinite possibilities.

Part of my job is team building activities. In a corporate set up team building can stimulate ideas, conversation and laughter while forging strong bonds within the team members. So start using some or all of these to create a closely knit, productive and happy team.
Those creative and brain storming sessions are not only vital to big companies, but can open up potentials for individual careers, however you can schedule them on your calendar between 10 and 12

on Thursdays and when you are not ready to open up they can suck the life out of your creativity.

So why is it only working during my creative workshops?

All it needs is a connection to that creative child within you that wants to come out and play.

Is the set up wrong?
It could be that she remains buried too deep under the weight of being serious.

Well during my long experience, I found out that no matter what reasons have contributed to your penned up creativity; it's not too late. By having little personal fun, you can learn to set your own potentials and creativity free.

The best part of my job in big companies is to share and help inspire a lot of people. It is a great fun when your boss schedules one of those brain storming sessions, and you get people to bring enough crayons and paper for everyone and share the fun.

Team building activities are highly important to enhance the productivity of a workforce. Unless a team is able to connect, it is difficult for them to reach out to each other with problems or queries. Therefore, an organization should concentrate on effective and fun team building activities that are effective both in terms of budget and time.

In fact, corporate team building ideas should be such that they should not only motivate the employees, but also give them a stock of beautiful memories.

Sometimes, my work in the companies is clouded with myth about the potential of creativity. People are often baffled over creativity and wonder where it comes from and where can we get more of it? What we do know for sure is that creativity is not some mystical magic that descends upon chosen people who are our creative superiors; it is in fact born within each of us and remains there until we die. All we have to do is set it free.

Among numerous fun and team building activities is a group painting activity for adults. This way, they learn to handle a job while cooperating with everyone.

First of all, we have to concentrate on the individual's uncorked potentials, intuition and creativity. Creativity and intuition are interdependent and intricately linked. Both flow through the same channels which connect you to something greater than yourself and beyond the realms of rational thought. It is the   source of all inspiration, radical insights, and innovation. Whenever you engage in any creative activity, you are strengthening your intuitive muscles and vice versa.
As you develop your intuition you also enhance your creativity as well.

The key is to clear up the channels through which your intuition and creativity flow. In doing so, solutions, inspiration, and ideas will come to you much more easily.

First step it's to clearing up your intuitive channels.

Have you ever noticed that while you're out walking, washing the dishes, meditating, exercising, or doing some kind of physical activity, ideas and solutions spontaneously pop up?
This is because your intuitive channels open up while you are fully engaged in the moment.
Your mind, your fears, and emotions momentarily get out of the way, allowing you to hear the messages from your intuition. These usually get drowned out by all the other noise inside your head.

Engaging in creative activities like painting, snapping photos with your phone, cooking, playing music, or doodling also has the same effects and the key is to be fully immersed in the moment. So let's start with opening up your intuitive and creative flow.

To help ease you into this process, here's a simple exercise you can do:
- Close your eyes and take 3 long deep breaths.
- With your eyes still closed; say to yourself:
"Creativity flows freely through me."
"I allow my intuition to guide me."
"There are no mistakes."

- Get a piece of paper and a pen: You can use anything you want to draw on, but a piece of scrap paper works best, as it is something that you aren't very attached to. This way, you will be more free and open when scribbling on it.

- Optional: Set a timer for 5-10 minutes.

- Pick up the pen and make a mark on the page. It can be anything. A circle, a squiggle, a line, a big blob. Whatever you feel like, just make a mark.

- Repeat to yourself again: "I allow my intuition to guide me... There are no mistakes."

- Now, starting from the mark you just made, begin doodling. Don't worry about what comes out. It can be anything. Just start scribbling whatever you feel like. Whatever wants to come out, let it out. Let it flow.
- Without judgment or thinking about what the final outcome will be, let the marks you make on the page flow naturally and effortlessly.
- Do this for a few minutes, and get yourself lost in the process.
- Whenever you start to feel yourself tensing up, repeat the phrases: "There are no mistakes... Creativity flows freely through me..."
- When the time is up, take a moment to review what you just created. What do you see? How does it make you feel? Is there something that speaks to you

in there? Or do you perhaps see nothing? Because that's totally fine, too.

- Pick the best part of your small drawing and set a rectangle around it. Divide this rectangle in vertical and horizontal halves. Do this again so that you have a grid.

- Draw the same grid only bigger on a big piece of paper or a canvas. One square after the next then transfer your small drawing into a big design.

- Now feel free to get into a creative mood with colors and patterns.

Tips:
If you are struggling with the free fun drawing; here's another way to proceed.

Borrow a composition: To make it easier on yourself, especially if you have a problem with composition and design, pick a favorite painting from an old master and look at its spatial divisions. Draw those shapes onto your paper.

Then pick an area and with your varied assortment of brushes; make some marks. When you really think about it, painting is all about making your own marks. Let each and every section dry before you go to the next.

Try glazing: You can select an area that you wish to glaze. Before you glaze, mask off parts of that area with frisket or tape. Apply a transparent glaze of one color over the area. Drop in other colors while the area is wet, if you wish. Let everything dry, move the tape and then repeat the process as many times as you wish. You'll be amazed at the variety of interesting looks and textures you can create!

Doing a messy painting is a dynamite exercise to teach you how paint works. If wonderful images emerge using this process, great! If not, you've got an interesting new surface to paint on.

Don't analyze or try to control what comes out. Just let the pen move instinctively on the page.

If it helps, make the marks quickly, so that your movements are more automatic and spontaneous.

The purpose of the exercise is to let go and loosen up. To give yourself a point of focus in which to lose yourself and begin to open up your intuitive and creative channels.

For now, the goal is to simply let go and have fun!

These personal play times are designed to help you learn to bring out your creativity and not just when you've marked it on the calendar. We get stuck because we trained ourselves that way. This free exercise helps bring us back to our young self, to a time when we didn't know what stuck was. The best thing is when you are connected to this free wild creative source there are not boundaries for interaction. Use art to get back in touch with the fun in creativity, and over time you'll find it gets easier and easier to use your creativity whenever you want.

Just as we all have intuition, we all have creative abilities. This is why children get so much delight out of art. When they have a pen in their hand, or anything to make a mark with they just go for it and have fun.

We are born to create. However, over time most of us lose our openness and playfulness when it comes to creating. At least when you throw the word "art" in there. Be rest assured you are full of creativity! Why not unleash it and tap in to your intuition at the same time?

Observe a child doing everyday activities and it's hard to miss that they bring creativity with them in everything they do, and everywhere they go. As adults, on the other hand, for some reason we feel the silly need to plan creative time as if, it wouldn't happen otherwise.

We can blame it on our tight schedules and overly committed lives, but the bottom line is planning for "creating creativity" is a bit like telling a creature,i.e. a tiger, that you'll feed it once a week and it's not allowed to be hungry beyond that. Under these circumstances a lion will probably do one of two things; eat your arm the first chance it gets or wither up and die.

<u>CONCLUSION</u>

BE
OUTSTANDING

Conclusively, it is the hope of the authors of this revealing book that each and every woman who reads the chapters of this book will come to realize that their search for more significance, a better quality of life, improved health and personal development can all be achieved through the practice of Yoga and art.

Do not be confined by your feelings, your current circumstances or even the opinion of your closest friends, light that fire within your soul and develop the drive and stamina to demolish everything that stands in your way. You may feel overwhelmed and defeated at times, but rest assured that each and every one of your dreams are valid. Now, it is your turn, go chase after them and be outstanding!

www.ingramcontent.com/pod-product-compliance
Lightning Source LLC
Chambersburg PA
CBHW070031210526
45170CB00012B/533